世界上最大的家庭
THE BIGGEST FAMILY
in the world

作者：保罗·H·博格　　绘画：费伊·昊勒　　前言：格瑞斯·穆图亚　　翻译：董一岩(Singh Dong)
Written by Paul H. Boge　　Illustrations by Faye Hall　　Foreword by Grace Mutua

The Biggest Family in the World
Copyright ©2015 Paul H Boge
All rights reserved
Original printing (English)—2015
Mandarin translations—2021

ISBN 978-1-927355-36-7 Soft Cover (English only)
ISBN 978-1-927355-37-4 Ebook (English only)
ISBN 978-1-988928-36-4 Soft Cover (Mandarin only)
ISBN 978-1-988928-38-8 Soft Cover (Mandarin/English version)
ISBN 978-1-988928-37-1 Ebook (Mandarin only)

Published by:
Castle Quay Books
Pickering, Ontario, L1W 1A5
Tel: (416) 573-3249
E-mail: info@castlequaybooks.com
www.castlequaybooks.com

Illustrations by Faye Hall
Proofread by Lori Mackay
Cover and book layout by Burst Impressions

Cataloguing in Publication information may be obtained from Library and Archives Canada.

CASTLE QUAY BOOKS

前言

在这个世界上，很少有人有机会拥有一位像我爸爸查理·穆利一样的父亲，在一个美好的一天，宣布你的生活将立刻被改变，因为他计划变卖掉他所有的生意和财产，而且将自己的一生致力于救助那些"最不想被人要的"街童！

当我们跟随并支持我们父母的呼召——救助那些孤儿和无助脆弱的儿童，彻底地改变了肯尼亚和整个非洲的小区，这样的生活对我和我的兄弟姐妹们来说确实是一个巨大的挑战。路程漫长，艰难且富有挑战；然而，当每一天我们看到一个新的孩子从生命受到威胁的情况下得到救助时，这让我们感到非常的欣慰和满足。我和我父母在《穆利之家》工作是我一生永不改变的事。

通过我父亲的一生，我懂得了聆听上帝呼召的价值，无论上帝引导我去哪里我都跟随他，甚至当危机来临不知如何处理的时候，我依然要依靠和信仰上帝。我已经在《穆利之家》学会了每天都要相信奇迹会发生！看着父亲的信心和信靠，上帝总是让人振奋不已！

这是我最深层次的祷告，还有希望本书能点亮阅读此书的每一位孩子的脸颊和心灵——让你们知道无论你的背景是什么，无论你来自哪里，无论你经历过多少苦难，盼望在我们的造物主手中。上帝会带领你走出最深的低谷，高举你，将你安置在高山之巅，因为你是珍贵的，你值得拥有充满喜乐、爱、尊重、和平，以及最重要的，高尚的人生。

—查尔斯·穆利和艾斯特·穆利的女儿，
格瑞斯·穆图亚。

FOREWORD

Few people in the world have an opportunity of having a father such as my dad, Dr. Charles M. Mulli, walk in on an otherwise beautiful day and declare that your life will change immediately as he plans on selling all his businesses and properties and dedicate his entire life savings to the rescue of the "most unwanted" street children!

Life has been such an adventure for my siblings and me as we follow and support our parents in their calling to rescue orphans and vulnerable children and transform communities across Kenya and Africa as a whole. The journey has been long, very tough and challenging; however, it has been most fulfilling as each day sees a new child's life saved from life-threatening situations. Working with my parents at the Mully Children's Family is one thing in life that I would not change for anything.

Through the life of my father, I have learned the value of listening to God's calling, following God no matter where He leads me, and trusting and believing in God even when there seems to be no possible solution to a crisis. I have learned to believe in miracles as that has become a daily occurrence at Mully Children's Family! Seeing Dad's faith and trust in God is always refreshing!

It is my deepest prayer and hope that this book will light up the face and heart of each and every child that touches it – to know that no matter your background, no matter where you come from, no matter the hardships you have gone through, there is hope in our Creator. God will take you from the deepest valley and lift you up above the highest mountain, for you are precious and deserving of a life filled with joy, love, respect, peace and above all, a life of dignity.

—*Grace Mutua, daughter of Charles and Esther Mulli*

在非洲美丽的天空下，在浩瀚、一望无际的肯尼亚，居住着一个贫穷的六岁男孩，他的名字叫查尔斯·穆利。

和很多其他孩子一样，穆利总是很孤单，在他的内心深处渴望自己能拥有一个家庭。

Under the beautiful African sky, in the vast landscape of Kenya, lived a poor six-year-old boy named Charles Mulli.

Like many other children, Mulli was all alone. Deep down inside, Mulli wanted to belong to a family.

当其他孩子走进教室的时候，穆利在旁边看着。他也想读书，但是他没有钱支付学费。当其他学生在学习的时候，穆利在想自己的人生会变成什么样子。

Mulli watched as the other children entered the classroom. He wanted to learn too, but he had no money and could not pay the school fees. While the other children studied, Mulli wondered what would become of his life.

晚上，穆利会把手放在他饥饿的肚子上，希望有吃的东西填满饥肠辘辘的肚子。

在早晨，他会鼓起勇气去要饭。当他伸手时，他的肚子咕咕叫，而其他的孩子们都看着他。

At night, Mulli would wrap his arms around his hungry stomach, hoping for something to fill his emptiness.

In the morning he would gather his courage to beg for food. His stomach growled as he held out his hands while the other children watched him.

多年以来，穆利在烈日下挖洞挣钱，这些钱只够支付食物和一个狭小的地方睡觉。

For years, Mulli dug holes under the hot sun to earn just enough money for food and a small place to sleep.

当穆利成长为一个少年时，一个朋友鼓励他："和我一起去教会吧。那里有一个特别的聚会。"

When Mulli became a teenager, a friend encouraged him, "Come to church with me. There is a special meeting taking place."

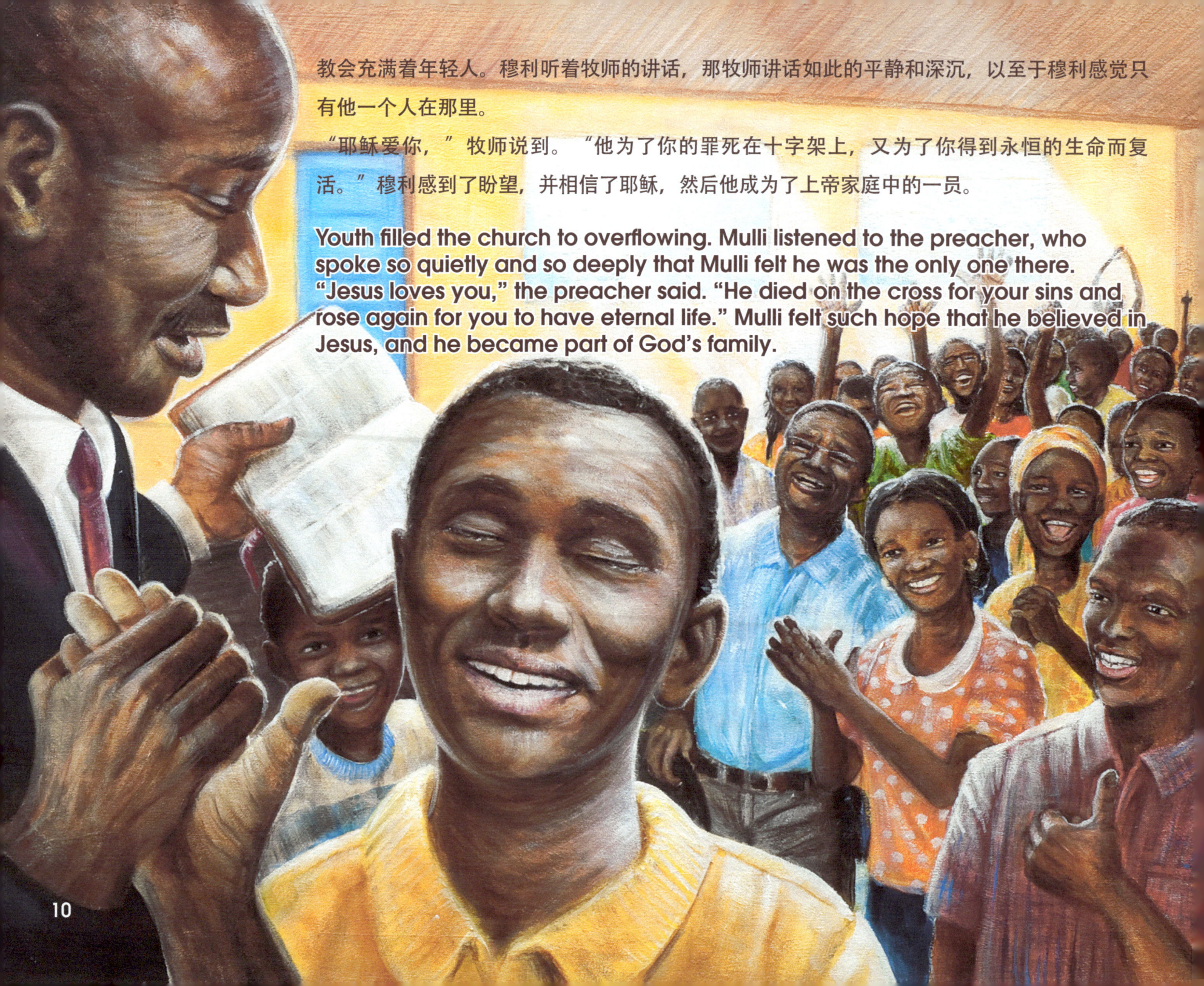

教会充满着年轻人。穆利听着牧师的讲话，那牧师讲话如此的平静和深沉，以至于穆利感觉只有他一个人在那里。

"耶稣爱你，"牧师说到。"他为了你的罪死在十字架上，又为了你得到永恒的生命而复活。"穆利感到了盼望，并相信了耶稣，然后他成为了上帝家庭中的一员。

Youth filled the church to overflowing. Mulli listened to the preacher, who spoke so quietly and so deeply that Mulli felt he was the only one there. "Jesus loves you," the preacher said. "He died on the cross for your sins and rose again for you to have eternal life." Mulli felt such hope that he believed in Jesus, and he became part of God's family.

这是第一次，穆利感受到了真正的喜乐。他内心充满着盼望。但他没上过学，没有钱，他也不认为自己有任何特殊的才能。所以他在心里疑惑："上帝啊，你到底想要在我身上做什么？"

几年后，穆利在田里干活，他遇见了一位名叫以斯帖的女人，他的心跳加速。当他见到她的那一刻，他爱上了她，而且不久之后她成为了穆利的妻子。

For the first time, Mulli felt true joy. His heart was full of hope. Still, he had no schooling and no money, and he did not think he had any special talents. So he wondered in his heart, "God, what do You want to do with me?"

A few years later while working in a field, Mulli's heart beat faster when he met a beautiful young woman named Esther. The moment he saw her, he loved her, and soon she became his wife.

11

穆利工作异常努力。从白天工作到深夜，他花了大量的时间在工作上。他开始了开出租车的小生意，这种出租车也被称为"马塔图"

很多人乘坐他的"马塔图"！

他的生意日渐壮大。他开展了其它的生意并且变得越来越富有。他挣了如此多的钱以至于可以买任何他想买的东西。

Mulli worked extremely hard. Long days. Late nights. Many, many hours. He started a small business driving a taxi, also called a *matatu*. A lot of people fit inside his *matatu*! His business grew bigger and bigger. He started other businesses and became richer and richer. He earned so much money that he could buy anything he wanted.

12

穆利和以斯帖喜欢和他们的八个很棒的孩子在一起共度时光：米里亚姆，格瑞斯，简，卡尔利，栋多，穆厄尼，艾萨克和迪克森。这是一个大家庭。

但他们的家庭将会变得更大！

大得多的多！

Mulli and Esther loved to spend time with their eight wonderful children – Miriam, Grace, Janey, Kaleli, Ndondo, Mueni, Isaac and Dickson. It was a big family.

But their family was about to become bigger.

A whole lot bigger!

13

穆利开着车来到了位于埃尔多雷特的一条街上，看见了很多穷孩子。他们穿着脏衣服，他们的眼神疲惫。没有家，没有食物，没有上学，而且没有希望。他们就像以前的穆利那样。

Mulli drove down a street in Eldoret and saw many poor children. Their clothes were dirty, their eyes tired. No home, no food, no school, and no hope. They were the same as he had been.

当其他穷孩子经过他的车，穆利的爱驱使着他为他们停留下来。

While others passed by, Mulli's love compelled him to stop for them.

14

穆利走出了他的汽车，把面包递给了饥饿的孩子们。

他们迅速地从他的手中拿走了面包。

"我们很久没吃东西了，"一个女孩说到，"我们也没有地方睡觉，你知道我们可以呆在哪里吗？"

Mulli stepped out of his car and gave bread to the hungry children. They quickly took it from his hands.

"We haven't eaten in a long time," a girl said. "And we have no place to sleep. Do you know where we can stay?"

15

这刺痛了穆利的心。"为什么有这么多孩子流浪街头?"他在想。"谁来帮助他们?"他把车停靠在一座桥边并祷告。

"噢,主啊,你给了我所有。你将我从最深的低谷带到了最高的山巅。但人生的目的只是为了钱吗?我把一切都交给你。"

This hurt Mulli. "Why are there so many children in the streets?" he wondered. "Who helps them?" He pulled over at a bridge and prayed.

"O God, You have given me everything. You have brought me up from the deepest valley to the highest mountaintop. But is money the only purpose of life? I turn everything over to You."

那天晚上穆利对他的家人们宣布："我正在变卖我们所有的一切财产，而且我将自己的一生致力于帮助在街上流浪的孩子们。"他们十分地惊讶，不知道接下来会发生什么。

That evening Mulli announced to his family, "I am selling everything we have, and I am dedicating my entire life to helping the street children." They were really, really surprised and wondered what would happen next.

穆利走进了肯尼亚的街道和贫民窟。他看到那么多需要帮助

的孩子，数量多得数不清。

Mulli walked into the streets and slums of Kenya.
He saw so many children who needed help that
he could not count them all.

穆利尽可能地把这些孩子带回家。他成为了孩子们的父亲，他们喜爱称呼他为爸爸。所以穆利把他们称为："穆利儿童之家"。

Mulli brought as many children as he could into his home. He became their father and they loved to call him Daddy. So he named them Mully Children's Family.

19

穆利为孩子们搭建了温暖舒适的床来安睡——一个可以被称为家的地方。一个能让他们的眼睛闪烁希望之光，让他们的心充满感恩的地方。穆利家庭逐渐壮大——从十一个孩子一直增加到四十个。

Mulli built beds for the children to have a cozy, warm place to sleep – a place to call home. A place where their eyes became bright with hope and their hearts full of thanks. Mulli's family grew bigger and bigger – from eleven children all the way to forty.

孩子们可以吃到饱。大豆和米饭还有芒果，以及一种特殊的玉米饭，类似于"粗玉米粥"。

穆利为了孩子们建造教室供他们学习，让他们成为上帝所要他们成为的人。医生，教师，工程师和牧师。

Mulli built classrooms for the children to study and become what they were designed to do. Doctors and teachers and engineers and pastors.

The children ate until they were full. Beans and rice and mangos and a special corn dish like porridge called *ugali*.

21

穆利家庭从四十个孩子成长到七十人，又增长到一百人！

Mulli's family grew from forty to seventy to one hundred children!

看着孩子们从街上流浪的旧生活转变为在耶稣里满怀希望的新生活，他喜欢看到孩子们的改变。"财富不是关于金钱。"穆利发现道，"财富是一个改变了的生命。"

He loved to see his children change from their old life on the street to having a new life with hope in Jesus. "Prosperity isn't about money," Mulli observed. "Prosperity is a changed life."

22

穆利变卖了自己最后的生意，土地还有汽车，把自己所有的钱都拿来供养他的孩子们。

Mulli sold the last of his businesses, land and cars and gave all his money to feed his children.

但有一天他们遇到了一个大问题——他们没有钱了，他们也没有吃的东西了。

But one day they faced a big problem – they ran out of money and they had nothing left to eat.

但他们仍然有希望。他们在上帝那里有希望。穆利和以斯帖彼此握着对方的手，开始一起祷告。"亲爱的上帝，即使这很困难，而且我们不知道怎么办，我们相信你会帮助我们。"然后…

But they still had hope.
They had hope in God.
Mulli and Esther held hands
and prayed together.
"Dear God, even though
this is very hard, and we
don't know what to do, we
have faith in You to help
us." And then…

25

他们听见有敲门声，他们赶紧跑下楼去…
They heard a knock at the door. They hurried downstairs...

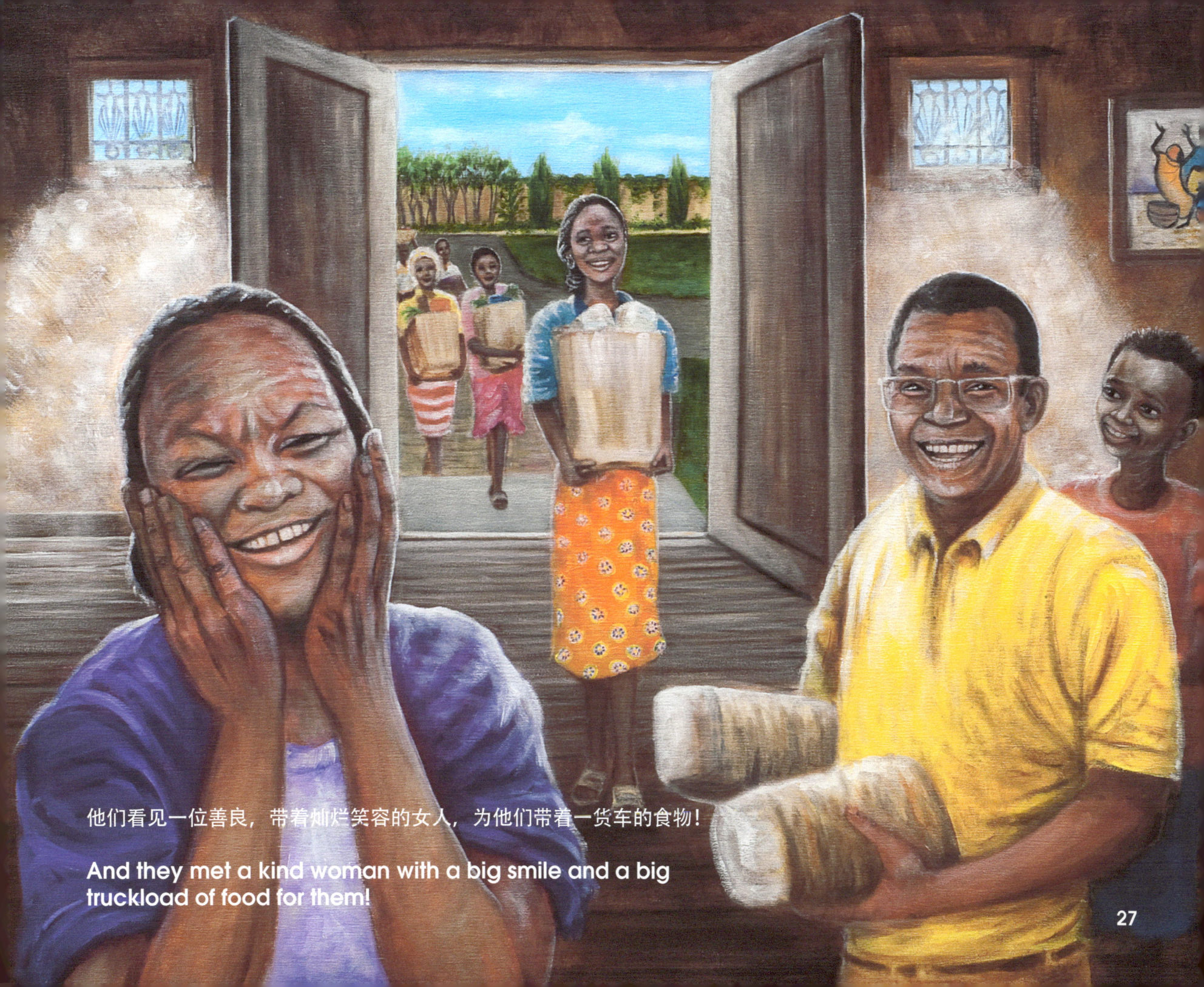

他们看见一位善良，带着灿烂笑容的女人，为他们带着一货车的食物！

And they met a kind woman with a big smile and a big truckload of food for them!

穆利家庭变得太大以至于没有更多的空间容纳孩子们。所以穆利带着孩子们离开自己的旧房子来到一块崭新的土地，是上帝呼召他们来的。这块遥远的地被称为纳达尔尼，他们将会在这里开始新的生活。

The family became so big that there was no more room. So Mulli led the children out of their old house to a brand new land where God had called them. A land far away called Ndalani, where they would start a new life together.

MCF
NDALANI

MULLY CHILDREN'S FA
WELCOM

即便他遇见许多冒险和挑战，穆利还是会花时间去笑，去倾听，去爱。

无论何时，当他的孩子们要来见穆利并且问他是否方便和他说话，穆利会说："我总有时间。"

Even with all his many adventures and all his many challenges, Mulli took time to laugh, to listen and to love.

Whenever one of his children would come to Mulli and ask if it would be possible to speak with him, Mulli would say, "There's always time."

在他们的新家他们面临着另一个大问题——他们没有水。孩子们变得非常口渴，穆利在思考如何让所有的孩子都能喝上干净的水。他能在哪里得到帮助呢？

At their new home they faced another big problem – they ran out of water. The children became so thirsty, and Mulli wondered how all his children would receive clean water to drink. *Where would he find help?*

31

穆利跪在地上然后很迫切地祷告。"噢，上帝啊，他们告诉我这里没有水。但你已经把我们领到这里了。请帮助我们。"

Mulli knelt down and prayed very long and very, very hard. "O God, they tell me there is no water here. But you have led us to this place. Please help us."

然后上帝对穆利说："快点站起来，带上你的妻子，我将告诉你哪里有水。"穆利和以斯帖急忙在夜里跑了出去。"在这里转弯，"上帝说。然后他们转了弯。"停在这儿"，上帝说。然后他们停住了。"这里有水。"

Then God spoke to Mulli: "Quick, stand up, take your wife, and I will show you where there is water." Mulli and Esther hurried outside into the night. "Turn here," God said. And they turned.

"Stop here," God said. And they stopped. "Here there is water."

突然…

Suddenly…

铲了又铲，工人换了一轮又一轮，他们
一直向下挖了两天。终于他们听见了令
人难以置信的声音。

Shovel by shovel. Worker by
worker. They dug down for
two days. Then they heard
something incredible.

33

一股巨大的喷泉从地下涌出，直冲云霄！

穆利、以斯帖和所有的孩子高兴地跳了起来！他们感觉到了清澈的水淋在他们身上，感谢上帝创造了又一个奇迹。

A huge gush of water sprang up from the ground and burst high into the sky!

Mulli, Esther and all the children jumped with joy! They felt the good, clean water fall down on them as they thanked the Lord for yet another miracle.

"耶稣给了我们生命的活水，"穆利说道。"他是生命的粮。如果你相信他，那么上帝会成为你天上的父，你也会成为他家庭的一员。"

"Jesus gives us living water," Mulli said. "He is the bread of life. If you believe in Him then God will be your heavenly Father and you will be part of His family."

那给了孩子们如此多的盼望，很多孩子们相信了耶稣。

That gave the children so much hope, and many put their trust in Jesus.

35

在美丽的非洲天空下，几百个穆利之家的孩子歌唱着。他们来自全肯尼亚不同的地方以及不同的部落。然而现在他们是一家人。一个拥有成千上万成员的家庭！"天父上帝，你真的完成了一件奇妙的工作，"穆利祷告道。"感谢你让我成为这家庭的一员。"

Hundreds of Mulli's children sang under the beautiful African sky. They had come from different places and different tribes throughout Kenya. And yet, they are one family. A family of thousands and thousands! "Father, You have really done an amazing work," Mulli prayed. "Thank You for letting me be part of this family."

36

穆利家庭还在继续成长。甚至有些人说他们是世界上最大的家庭！想一想这所有一切都开始于一个孩子聆听了上帝的声音。

那么你呢？你将会成为什么样的人？你是否可以对上帝说：“你想对我做什么？”

The family continues to grow. Some even say they are the biggest family in the world! And to think it all started with one child listening to God. So what about you? Who will you grow up to be? Can you say to God, "What do You want to do with me?"

非洲

肯尼亚

提问：

1. 当你没有东西吃的时候，你是什么感受？
2. 如果你有很多钱的时候，你会干什么？
3. 当你生活在这么大的一个家庭里，你的感受是什么？
4. 谈一谈你感到孤独和被冷落的一次经历。
5. 穆利帮助了许多的孩子们并成为他家庭的一份子。

   对于你周边寻找心灵寄托的其他人，你能做什么帮助他们呢？
6. 你是否有什么办法帮助那些穷人？
7. 谈论一次你为了某事向上帝祷告的经历。
8. 你是否要求过让耶稣来宽恕你，相信他并成为他家庭的一员？

发音指导（文中出现的人名和地名）：

Kaleli：卡雷利

Matatu：玛塔图

Mueni：美尼

Mulli：穆利

Mully：穆利

Nadalani：拿大拉尼

Ndondo：恩多恩多

Ugali：欧伽利

定义

繁荣、成功

贴士：

穆利（Mulli）是他姓氏。当所指为"穆利儿童之家"时使用穆利（Mully）。

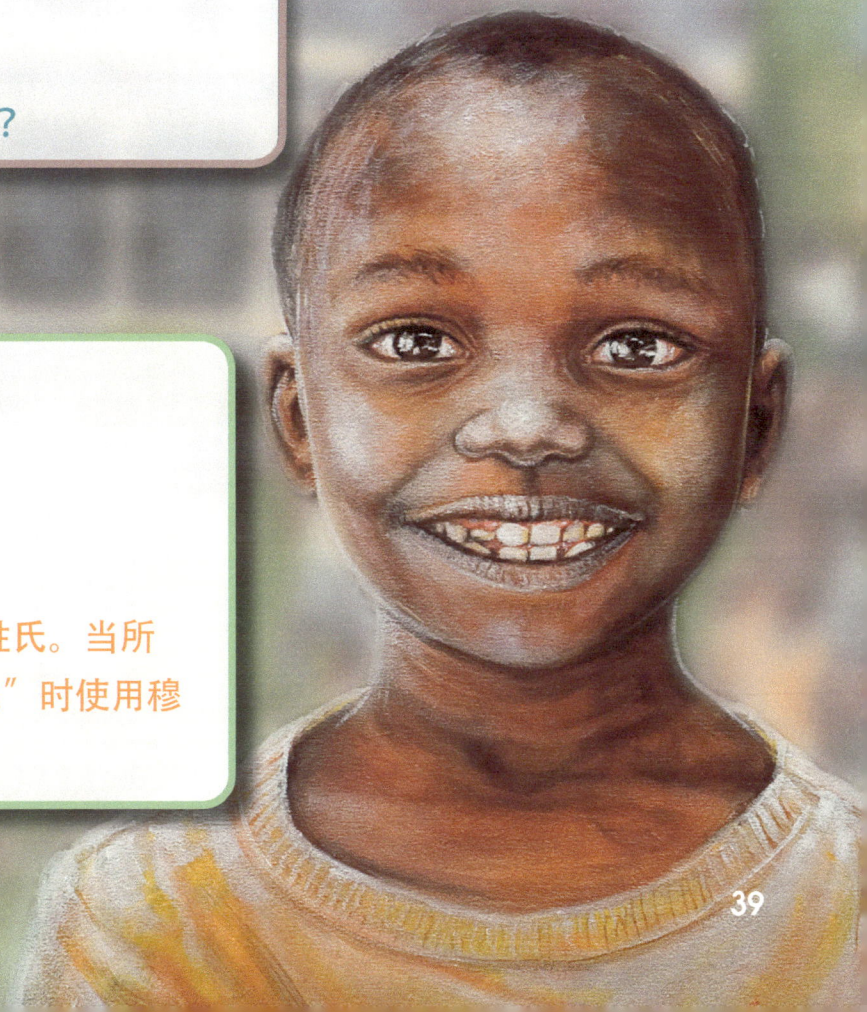

39

想了解更多信息请访问：
www.MullyChildrensFamily.org